Dedication

This project is dedicated to everyone who has been saved by music.

If this book means something to you, I'd love to know. Questions/comments can be sent to hopejacobsonstory@gmail.com

Preface

This is an unfiltered collection of life stories, some sad, some joyful, and most a mixture of the two. Hopefully, my experiences show how strong the power of music can be, especially for people who live with mental illnesses and/or Autism. I also hope that my descriptions show how intense my sensory system is hit by certain songs, some in ways that are hard to explain and others in ways that led to the creation of memorable moments.

I was admittedly hesitant to share this book with the world, but I'm at a strong enough place mentally where I can see why I struggle: so that others do not have to experience the same hardships. It would be a disregard of my life's purpose if I did not share my story to help de-stigmatize conversations regarding mental health and remind others that recalling certain people, places, and events with a mixed bag of emotions is normal and valid. I hope to express authentic emotions and reactions in order to remind readers that there is strength in vulnerability.

I do not intend to distinguish which stories relate more to my Autism compared to which ones are more associated with anxiety. My main point is to tell my stories without shielding any part of my identity, but also without making any part of my identity seem like my whole self. Whether I ought to attribute certain experiences to my Autism, my anxiety, or other issues is beside the point. I am fully human with stories to share that cannot be narrowed down to definitions of mental conditions.

One final point that I must address: some of the stories in this book contain heavy subject matter to remain authentic. I understand that reading about certain experiences can create flashbacks and/or relapses for those struggling with eating disorders, depression, and/or coping with the loss of loved ones. Therefore, I will have a "Trigger Warning" message before each story that contains material that should be read at your own discretion. I am not promoting negative thoughts and behaviors, but I am intentionally including my experiences with them in this book, in the hopes that my honesty inspires others to seek the necessary help to address any concerning thoughts and behaviors they see in themselves.

Disclaimer

The following stories reference real people and their actions, but names have been changed for the sake of privacy.

<u>Part One: The Elementary School Years</u>

B.O.B. Featuring Rivers Cuomo, "Magic" I first heard this song in elementary school, a time when I still got nervous even at the thought of someone saying hi to me. For me to reveal something about myself as personal as my favorite song? Unthinkable! But "Magic" made me feel like I was bouncing up and down when I actually remained still, and the sensation was so thrilling that I told someone about a song I liked for the very first time. After playing it for my brother, he simply said "not bad," and I spent several hours worrying about that. Was that the nice way to avoid saying my music taste sucks? Or did he honestly mean it was just an okay song? Either way, where was the enthusiasm?! Was it weird for me to be fascinated by the emotional impact of a song? Was it odd to feel a song with every fiber of my being and get taken to another place mentally while listening to it?

Evanescence Featuring Paul McCoy, "Bring Me to Life" There is something about the mix of pitch, instruments, and overall eerie qualities in this song that always makes me feel like a fan is blowing in my face, like there is a force pushing against me from which I cannot escape. The first time I heard this song in its entirety was at a school assembly. The song was part of a playlist that blasted as students and staff entered the room, yet a student in the front row of the bleachers still managed to fall asleep before the presentation had even started. The guest speaker walked over to the student and yelled "WAKE ME UP!" at the same time as the singer did, causing me to feel like I had been pushed backwards. He woke up the student on the first try, yet the speaker seemed so amused that he proceeded to chant "WAKE ME UP!" in the student's face every time the singer did in the chorus. Everyone witnessing this spectacle laughed except for me. I still don't know how I contained myself; I was close to boiling over with rage every time the speaker and audience members laughed at the gag. Why were they finding it so amusing to jolt awake students in this way and cause me to feel physically pushed with every chant? And how was I the only person who couldn't laugh this off? Was no one else having a minor panic attack every time he yelled? Was anyone going to ask if I was okay, or was I not visibly showing my feelings of nausea?

***High School Musical* Cast, the *High School Musical 2* Soundtrack** The third graders at my school, including me, were so obsessed with *High School Musical 2* that a large group of us decided to put on our own play based on the movie. We spent our recesses at "practice," debating everything from where to perform to how big our audience should be to what movie scenes would be cut from our production. We rehearsed songs in a big circle around the swing sets. Hopefully this was clear right off the bat, but just to be extra sure that I make my point, I outright REJECT all claims that a group of third graders singing together is likely to be on-key and have the same therapeutic qualities on me as listening to the original version of a song. But nevertheless, focusing on the songs from my favorite soundtrack helped turn up the radio versions of them in my mind, so I still found it joyful to hear everyone perform together.

Katie, the "ultimate cool girl" of my school, instantly became the director of the play. She suggested that all participants go over to her house for the "dress rehearsal" before the day of our show. I was thrilled because although my daily schedule would need alterations (something that gave me the urge to whimper in fear from feeling thrown off-balance), I was going to do something I truly found fun, and I was being invited to a house as if I was someone's friend! I had heard many invitations over the years from friends asking each other on "playdates" but had never been invited, so this was a huge deal to me.

Katie called me on the day of the "dress rehearsal" and said there had been a last-minute change: everyone should bring their swimsuits so we could swim in her pool during breaks. That didn't change anything for me, since I knew I would be too shy to wear a swimsuit in front of everybody, let alone change into it there. I showed up without one and decided I would just spend the five-minute breaks off in a corner on my own. After all, an excuse to step away from a crowd was one of my key strategies for avoiding a panic attack.

The afternoon left me crushed from the minute I arrived. By the time I showed up, everyone was swimming in the pool and taking turns on the waterslide. Music was playing on a boombox, but it was so loud that it sounded like static more than melodic noise to me. I felt too rattled by the music and unexpected circumstances to say much, so I just decided to go to a corner and wait for the rehearsal to start.

That time never came. Three hours of my head aching to the point of numbness later, Katie shrugged and decided she had "gotten over it." I didn't pick up on figures of speech quickly at this age, so it took me until I was walking home to realize that Katie had meant the play had been cancelled. I had experienced three hours of my life feeling physically rattled by music that sounded like static and had gotten my hopes up over starting a friendship over nothing.

**Ke$ha, "Blind"** During my rebellious, "I'm going to listen to tons of Ke$ha music without telling my parents!" phase at around age eight, I played this song on a loop. It's about telling an ex-lover "You'll be sorry you left me! You're going to miss me!" However, I interpreted it as a song about yelling at anyone by whom you felt wronged. Playing it made me feel like I was confidently striding up to Katie and ready to make her sorry (this was about more than just the play; there had been a long history of her putting me in other situations where I was left isolated in a corner while everyone else had the time of their lives together).

Miley Cyrus, "Seven Things" The music video for this song was one a group of Katie's friends and I watched on Katie's laptop during her sleepover. I remember letting that moment sink in as I felt disbelief; I had not only been invited to somebody's house, but it was *Katie's* house! Someone as cool as Katie wanting to get to know me better was my first memory of having confidence. That didn't last long.

Things I said and did at the sleepover were unfavorable in Katie's eyes; I had nothing to contribute to Truth-or-Dare (I got too self-conscious to pick either option), I voted to not watch a scary movie (due to getting startled in my daily life by so much as a doorbell ringing), and I asked what the schedule was (assuming that everyone lived life by self-made rules like I did). Katie had tried to "change the nerd" in me for months, but her subtle ways of trying to make me uncomfortable about my hobbies (such as playing with dolls) and trying to make me follow her lead (such as by starting to date other eight-year-olds) had fallen on deaf ears.

Katie's sleepovers went from including me to intentionally excluding me and making sure I noticed. She enjoyed loudly inviting people standing right next to me to her house, and then they would both start loudly gushing about all the fun they would have together.

Katie also made sure that I kept my "outcast" status by convincing her friends (which consisted of at least half of the third grade) to stop associating with me too. They all shoved their bags and books on the cafeteria benches so there was no spot for me to sit down next to them. Even when I did try to squeeze in, no one would budge to give me more than the smallest possible end of the bench. They also refused to give validity to a word I said; if I added a comment or question to the dialogue, they all fell silent in unison and looked at anything but me until someone else changed the subject. Eventually, Katie got her friends (yes, she was too scared to do it in person) to angrily storm up to me at recess, circle the swingset I was on alone, and ask, "Why are you still sitting with us when we're, like, all best friends, and you're just, like… there?"

I don't remember how I reacted because the wires in my brain felt like they were getting hooked up inaccurately. Not only did hearing that I was disliked by those I had considered my best friends leave me shaken, but so did the feeling of claustrophobia I got from being surrounded by half of the third grade. I can't listen to a single Miley Cyrus throwback now without feeling resentment and having flashbacks to the times I was made to feel worthless by Katie and her clique.

Miranda Cosgrove, "Kissing You" I remember magazine-hunting in a grocery store alone one day and hearing this song. It is a moment that I remember because it was a rare time where I felt proud of myself for going out in public by choice. Typically, I could not even walk down my driveway to get the mail without feeling self-conscious, but finding a magazine with a favorite musician on it was enough motivation to get me to go. I encourage everyone who has anxiety in public places to pat themselves on the back each time they go out; these instances of conquering anxiety are only *minor* victories if they are labeled as such, and there is no reason to do so!

Nitty Gritty Dirt Band, "Fishing in the Dark" My first dance recital, when I was four, involved a tap routine to this song. I dealt with selective mutism in those early years of my life (meaning that I could talk in certain places but went mute in others, such as in dance class and on stage), so I just did on stage what I did in the dance studio: stood there, looked at the floor, thought whatever the G-rated version of "WTF am I doing here?" is repeatedly in my head, and tried hard not to think about the bright lights, the thundering noise of tap shoes ringing in my head, and everybody staring at me.

Robosoul, "Masquerade" This is from the TV movie *Rags*, which my sister and I used to watch constantly. Whenever I was too busy to watch the full movie with her and "Masquerade" started playing, my sister called me so that I at least wouldn't miss that scene. This song was added to my Sensory Overload Prevention Playlist. It made me feel like my bones were all vibrating, but not in a scary way. It was more like a euphoric version of an electric shock.

Rush, "Roll the Bones" It took me many years to recognize and comprehend sarcasm and exaggerations, and I had no knowledge in this area at age seven. My dad was watching a Rush concert video and told me "an actual skeleton" was about to come on stage to sing part of the song. I was SO excited to see a literal skeleton perform live! When it turned out to be a computer-generated image on a screen, I felt not only betrayed, but ashamed of my ignorance.

The Black-Eyed Peas, "Meet Me Halfway" The first New Year's Eve that I decided to stay up until midnight was the year The Black-Eyed Peas performed this on a live New Year's Eve show. It was a rare occasion where I felt bold enough to break my schedule and stay up past my bedtime; winter break had helped me refill my social bank account from alone time, and that time created my willingness to be more flexible about my schedule. I was not allowed to go to any New Year's Eve parties, though. I assumed there was music playing at those parties, which might have delayed a panic attack, but my parents still thought the noise would be too overwhelming. Given the breakdown resulting from just watching fireworks on TV on that New Year's Eve, they were probably right.

U2, "Sometimes You Can't Make it On Your Own" I have always viewed changes both big and small as worth fearing, so to stop the feeling that everything was always changing, I decided to create some absolute truths in my life. I decided that my favorite color would always be pink, my favorite animal would always be a dog, and my favorite song would always be "Sometimes You Can't Make It On Your Own" by U2. Shockingly, all three of these favorites *have* changed. I tried very hard to resist changing my favorite things, always telling myself when I heard a new song that it wasn't as good as U2's song. It is a ground-out-from-under-me feeling when I verbally confirm a change in my life, and that was the case the day I finally admitted out that the U2 song had gotten boring.

<u>Part Two: The Middle School Years</u>

Introduction

Katie moved away by the time I entered middle school, but her being out of my life did not mean that my next attempts at friendships were any smoother. In the middle school cafeteria, I sat with a group of girls who were hard to read (the main one you will read about is Chelsea). I couldn't tell when they were making fun of me and when they were just playfully teasing. I did not know whether the ways they got me to do what they wanted were normal or abnormal, having had little experience in friendships. I did not have awareness of what behavior constitutes a "that's what friends are for" response and what crosses a line.

Chelsea and her friends laughed at and made comments about my outfits and hairstyles that were not directly compliments or insults (I apparently looked like Medusa when I put my frizzy hair in a high ponytail). They made jokes about how much of a "kiss-up" to teachers I came across as, and they even tested my goody-two-shoes nature by forcing me to break school rules during recess. They did things like making me play "Stabberscotch" (don't ask) despite my sheer terror and twisting my arms back until I felt like they would break, refusing to release me until I said a swear word.

The most uncomfortable out of all my memories with them was the time they showed up on my doorstep without warning. They jokingly said something along the lines of "we've got our eyes on you" earlier that day, and it was apparently hilarious for them to actually show up and prove they were watching me.

Aside from awkward attempts at friendships, my middle school years were full of darkness for many other reasons. Trouble getting to sleep, nightmares, OCD rituals, and perfectionistic tendencies took over my mind. I spent my free time re-writing homework assignments when I felt like my handwriting wasn't good enough, and I studied every spare moment of every day. I based my self-worth on my academic life, as if to compensate for where my social life was lacking.

I also sought validation through my appearance, as negative comments about looks become a more and more frequent topic of complaints among students. Self-loathing and comparing ourselves to others were norms. Like everything else I did, I took this norm to the max, as a way of both fitting in and distracting myself from my anxiety-filled days throughout these three years of my life.

Big Time Rush, "Invisible" Seeing Big Time Rush was my very first concert, making it a memorable roller coaster. I remember their performance of "Invisible" especially well because that was when I felt such a sensory overload that despite having the time of my life, I needed a break from it. I spent the song outside of the stadium, trying to figure out how to put in my ear plugs.

I returned to my seat in the arena and made it through the rest of the night without panicking, which gave me so much on which to reflect. I really could have fun *and* openly address and deal with severe anxiety?! I could feel the incredible sensations that good music brings me while in the midst of so much sensory input and so many people?! I could even start up conversations about music with fellow fans?! It was the most thrilling sense of connection. I found out right from my very first concert experience that despite having my anxiety triggered by crowds and loud noises, a concert environment is such an adrenaline rush that it pushes away all the negative voices in my head and turns the volume off on things that would otherwise distract and me and cause discomfort. Being connected to so many intense factors of the external world in a way that was not overwhelming was and still is remarkable to me; I finally found a place where I felt like my inner and outer worlds converged. I was surrounded by people who connected to the same music as me, making me feel a sense of belonging.

Billy Joel, "We Didn't Start the Fire" My seventh grade teacher decided to mix up her standard lesson plan and teach us history via song repetition instead of note-taking. She made us spend an entire class period researching the historical topics mentioned in "We Didn't Start the Fire" as she played the song again and again. AND AGAIN. AND AGAIN. FOR THE ENTIRE CLASS PERIOD. While some songs on a loop bring me a sense of calm from the repetition, this song just felt like someone was running in circles around me and shouting phrase after phrase in my ears. The teacher smiled the whole time, either because she had a next-level obsession with the song or because she enjoyed the shock and anger on students' faces. On the plus side, that class taught me I can still zone in on an assignment and get it done when my environment is overwhelming.

Fun., "We Are Young" I used to constantly write songs, oftentimes parodies instead of purely original works. I was exceptionally proud when I composed a version of "We Are Young" called "We Are Old." It was the exact same song, but I changed a bunch of the words into their opposites. For example, instead of setting the world on fire, I sang about filling the world with water. I was so proud of my musical masterpiece that I unconsciously started singing my remix while I was in the same room as my sister. Being only eight years old at the time, she found it as hilarious as I did, and while it initially felt exciting to get praise, the feeling quickly turned to dread. Whether we were at home or in public, no matter how few or how many people were watching, at every opportunity for several weeks, my sister belted out my remix and let everyone know I had written it. Saying that I was mortified would be an understatement. After weeks of unwanted attention being drawn toward me, I promised myself to make sure I never started singing in front of others again.

Judy Garland, "Somewhere Over the Rainbow"
Trigger Warning: This story briefly references eating disorder traits and suicide.

A motivational speaker spoke out against bullying at my middle school, and it was anything but expected. It truly made for one of the most memorable and impactful afternoons of my life. After telling stories of students who committed suicide after being bullied, the speaker said "Someone please get off the bleachers and over by me to apologize. Because I'm sure someone here bullied someone else in the past. I'll just sit here as long as it takes until someone comes down."

There was at least two minutes of awkward squirming before someone went down to the microphone. The student did not confess to any bullying but did apologize to someone for never being welcoming because seeing someone unwillingly alone and ignoring that is a form of bullying. The boy who had gotten an apology went down to the mic to thank the student, and they had an awkward hug.

There were a few more minutes of silence, then a girl went down to the microphone and made a similar apology. This was followed by another thank-you and embrace between students.

The breaks between students going to the microphone to apologize got shorter and shorter, and the hugs came across as more and more genuine. An hour flew by with more students apologizing and forgiving one another, and not just within friend groups, but also between the most unexpected combinations of students. By the end of the assembly, I knew the names of more students than ever before, and I really saw some of them for the first time, in every meaning of the word.

What shocked me the most was that the inside of my mind during the assembly was unusually quiet. I had so much to process in my external environment that it was all-consuming. I sometimes feel the emotions of the others in the room as strongly as if they were my own, and I felt every moment of regret, sorrow, and relief.

I felt like I was watching an immersive movie, so when one of the last speakers said my name, I snapped into reality and felt stunned. *Me? I* was permitted an apology for being ignored all these years too?

By the microphone, I joined the girl who had said my name and had apologized for allowing my isolation to continue. I had never felt so exposed as I did while standing there as she finished what she was saying and the entire student body stared at me. I was desperate to know if they not only saw me, but if they *saw* me.

Eighth grade had been the hardest year of my life up to this point; on top of the daily struggles I had been facing for as long as I can remember, I had developed severe Anorexia. My eyes were puffy, my hair was likely a mess, and my clothes looked oversized and disheveled. Did they see past all that and see *me*? Did they see someone they would remember? Did I even want them to, when invisibility and concealment had been my shields all my life so far?

The biggest question of all in my mind: why didn't I feel like running out of the gym in that moment? Why was I able to tolerate not one, not two, but hundreds of pairs of eyes seeing me? Maybe it was because I could sense everyone's emotions, and in that moment, I sensed honest remorse and compassion, things I never expected to sense in any of my peers.

The constant radio in my head remained turned off until the speaker made some closing remarks about how oddly easy it had been to reach out to one another once the initial awkwardness faded away. We all left the room while "Somewhere Over the Rainbow" played through the gym's speakers, and the hugging and apologizing continued. I don't remember how much I returned the eye contact and hugs I got from others, but I do remember sensing no false remorse from any of them. It was an incredibly trusting and open time for all of us.

LMFAO, "Party Rock Anthem"
Trigger Warning: This story discusses eating disorder traits and behaviors.

Eighth grade was the year where my disordered eating transformed into full-fledged Anorexia and my distorted, depressed thoughts filled my daily life. I was pissed off at everyone who tried to talk to me. My irritability stemmed from weight loss side effects (hair falling out in clumps, fatigue, dizzy spells, and being chilled to the bone, just to name a few), as well as the combination of anxiety and paranoia that fed into every choice I made. I assumed that my life would forevermore consist of exercising nearly every waking moment and eating as little as possible, so I thought my pissed-off mood would turn into a permanent personality trait. This just added to the depressed thoughts I had daily.

My one sense of salvation came from listening to music and going to dance classes; the one time no one nagged me to eat something or yelled at me after discovering one of my dangerous habits was when I went to dance class.

However, even my dance class was no longer a light in my life after a while, since my teacher decided the routine we would be practicing for the entire hours every class period would be set to the song "Party Rock Anthem." Something as little as being tired of hearing a song set me off during this time, so I intentionally messed up the group dance and stormed out of the room after each class, fuming to myself for hours afterwards over what a bitch my teacher was for making class no longer fun.

A few dance classes and a few hundred rounds of listening to "Party Rock Anthem" later, I quit dance class, among other activities that took time away from my eating-disorder-based rituals.

Michael Jackson, "Black or White" I performed a hip-hop dance routine to this years ago. This recital stood out more than others because of the way I acted. To be blunt, I was a total bitch.

I was more nervous for this show than I had been for past ones, which was odd, considering that I only had to interact with four other dancers in my class and had worked with twenty others in past classes. Whatever the reason, I was even more nervous and shy than usual on the day of the show. The four other dancers in my group chatted with each other in our dressing room, while I sat in the far corner. I didn't say a word to them, and I spent the entire time we were in there either practicing the routine on my own or re-doing parts of my hairstyle while staring at myself in the mirror. Eye contact felt like it was going to burn my skin today, rather than just make me squirm, so I stared at myself in the mirror for over an hour.

After our performance, it was my job to stay on stage while everyone else had danced off, so that I could twirl around the parachute under which a group of young ballerinas was hiding. Their routine started right after I pulled the parachute off of them and leapt offstage. My classmates waited for me in the wings, and as everyone applauded and I danced offstage, my classmates congratulated me and said I did a great job. I was so flustered from all the eyes I had felt stares from and so tired of being around so many people backstage all day that I couldn't fully register what they were saying. I had too much sensory input to keep a conversation going, so I just said "Yeah" and ran backstage without them.

I spent the rest of the show back in the dressing room, staring at myself. I *really* couldn't show my face now, after responding to a comment that implied a "thank you!" with "Yeah"!

My parents got mad at me when I admitted to not having said goodbye to anyone. I don't remember my response, but I do remember being absolutely livid. On the inside, I was ranting about how hard this day had been and how frustrating it felt when the day's struggles didn't even seem worth it. I was always scolded for what I *hadn't* done and never given credit for what I *had* done. Did anyone realize how fucking difficult it was to get myself to go to talk to my fellow dancers in class every week, let along at this fucking recital?!

Probably not, actually. I was on irritable rants often, but only in my head. Externally, I probably looked as calm as can be and said nothing on the car ride home but "Yeah."

Mitchel Musso, "The In Crowd" One summer, Chelsea suggested that she host her birthday party at my house, and she would turn it into a joint birthday party for both me and her (my birthday was just a month after hers). Being nervous asking my parents for anything ever, nervous at the thought of a party in my house, and nervous about what would happen to me physically or verbally if I said no caused me to say yes. Chelsea called my mom to spring the news on her and start planning. My mom likely went along with it both because she felt too uncomfortable to say no to Chelsea and because she was pleasantly surprised any time that I planned to hang out with someone outside of school hours.

I could write an entire book describing all the chaotic incidents that the birthday party included, but I'll just summarize what happened here: Chelsea came over and set up the decorations she bought, looked at the cake she had me get for her, and waited for the guests she had invited to arrive. When they all showed up, Chelsea's mom took us to a bowling alley and the arcade. At this point in my story, I don't see a need to explain my reactions again to environments like those. Unsurprisingly, I hid in the bathroom and panicked in both locations.

When we were dropped back off at my house, the night consisted of having the pizza and cake my family had bought for Chelsea, watching movies that Chelsea picked, being forced to play Truth-or-Dare, locking myself in a bathroom as everyone yelled at me to not be such a "scaredy-cat" during movies, being forced into a pillow fight that involved more heavy cushions than it did pillows, and Chelsea leaving the next morning without so much as a thank-you note.

As hard as it can be for me to pick up on social cues, anyone could see by this point that I was not in a true friendship and was being manipulated. I spent the post-sleepover day with a sharp headache as sounds kept repeating in my head of bowling pins, arcade games, yelling, singing, blowing up balloons, ripping open gifts...And don't get me started on how my senses of sight and smell were also overwhelmed.

On the post-sleepover night, I listened to "The In Crowd" on repeat. I hadn't listened to it in years but suddenly had the urge to because of how relatable the song felt as I thought about my attempts at friendships. The song still brings comfort to me and feels like my diary entry.

Zendaya, "Swag it Out" Frankly, family vacations make me nervous as fuck. Spending tons of time trying new things, seeing unfamiliar places, being around tons of people, sharing a bedroom and therefore having zero privacy, and being forced to go face the world when I just want to prevent a panic attack and stay in the hotel are what form my version of Hell. After each incredibly long day of Hell in Florida, I went on the hotel room's balcony and journaled while listening to "Swag it Out." At the time, it wasn't a silly song, but a badass one. A lot of Ke$ha music was also played that weekend. I had the urge to be "rebellious" and do something to "get back at" my parents for putting me through this ordeal. Lip-synching about wanting to be "where the freaks all come around" never felt so good.

<u>Part Three: The Big Breakdown</u>

Trigger Warning: This story contains specific eating disorder-rooted thoughts.

I had a mental breakdown in eighth grade that finally pushed into my consciousness how harmful my thoughts and actions had been towards myself over the years. I voluntarily checked myself into an eating disorder treatment center for six months, where I openly addressed Body Dysmorphic Disorder, anxiety, and an array of self-destructive behaviors I won't go into here (I am considering publishing a memoir specifically about this aspect of my life someday). The following songs played on my phone and the program members' phones most often during our downtime at the hospital. They may seem random, but they are each special to me for being the soundtrack to everything from meals that turned into screaming matches to peaceful days when we all bonded and boosted each other's self-esteem. They became the soundtrack in my mind during the downtime I used to reflect on both the lowest lows and the highest highs I witnessed, moments when one of us wanted everyone to fuck off and was nearly forced into having a feeding tube (including me), but also moments when one of us cried tears of joy over being discharged from the program and regaining a sense of purpose (also including me). These songs all make up my life-saving experience of seeing and being a part of humanity at its most intense:

Adele, "Set Fire to the Rain"
Adele, "Someone Like You"
Demi Lovato's entire discography
Drake Featuring Rihanna, "Take Care"
Gavin DeGraw, "Not Over You"
Greyson Chance, "Hold on 'Til the Night"

Hot Chelle Rae, "I Like it Like That"
Hot Chelle Rae, "Tonight Tonight"
Katy Perry, "Part of Me"
One Direction, "Little Things"

Eating disorders are never a passing trait; the roots of them can be recognized through therapy, but that doesn't eliminate those root causes. For example, my years of harassment at school, painful shyness, the urge for perfectionism that I could never attain, and severe anxiety led me to crave a sense of control over my life, which I found by controlling my appearance. Rewiring my thought processes to recognize the damage my thoughts caused me did not get rid of my need for control. This made my high school years, which were also my post-hospitalization recovery years, so difficult. I now knew which coping mechanisms would literally kill me, but I still needed to find and practice healthy replacements. Anxiety took center stage throughout my high school experiences, which is when I felt more strongly in-tune with my physical reactions to music than ever before and worked on finding out which music would help me find at least some fleeting moments of inner peace.

Part Four: The High School Years

Here is what a day in my life during high school was like:

I wake up after either a nightmare or just another restless sleep. I fear getting out of bed and facing the day, not for any reasons with deep, philosophical meaning, but simply because I don't want to leave the warmth of my comforter. I feel the air conditioning intensely, as if I were outside in January. Eventually, I force myself out of bed and start my morning routine. If I'm lucky, my sister is following her routine too, but if not, she'll be hogging the bathroom and messing up my schedule. At exactly 6:21a.m., I need to enter the bathroom, so when she doesn't let me in and the clock moves on to 6:22 a.m., I start nervously whimpering and pacing, feeling like the world is about to end. At 6:23 a.m., my sister opens the bathroom door to let me in; my whimpering does not take long to get on her nerves (although that minute always feels like an eternity for me).

I take the bus to school and try to use whatever minimal sunlight comes through the windows to do some studying as a distraction from the loudness and rowdiness.

I go to my locker while talking to my brother to try distracting myself from the fact that I'm walking through loud and crowded hallways. I hope that none of my classmates go to my locker to chat before class; I don't know how to respond even to a question as seemingly surface-level as "How was your weekend?" My one exception besides my brother, however, is Aidan. Aidan periodically says hi to me at my locker, and I can actually reply with more than a yes or a no. I feel unusually comfortable around Aidan; he has never revealed an Autism Spectrum or anxiety disorder diagnosis, but we certainly share many personality traits.

I make it through my classes as best as I can, despite stuttering and sweating and shaking and overall being a nervous wreck when I have to speak in front of the class. I spend lunch in the nurse's office, a short but much-needed reprieve.

The rest of my day is a mirror image of the morning: I get distracted and flustered easily in my classes but somehow make it through them, I don't willingly converse with anyone I see in the hallways (except for Aidan), I take a noisy bus ride home, and then I work for hours to distract myself. I force myself to take a mental breather and calm down before bed by listening to music, which is truly my salvation. Then, I go to bed and take a long time to fall asleep, both due to a racing mind and the fear of sleep itself. My dreams and nightmares are equally vivid and layered, full of both friendly and traumatizing imagery, and I never know when I shut my eyes which ones I'll have to face.

Alt-J, "Breezeblocks" I really enjoyed this song and video… at first. The sheer strangeness of its sound and video concept intrigued me, and anything that can get my *full* attention is a noteworthy rarity. I also loved the way the song made me feel, as if my live-wire nerves were being pinched one-by-one throughout the song, not in a painful way but a numbing one. The bridge in the song removed some of the numbness and made me feel excited, for what I do not know. It was as if the first half of the song was my anesthesia that prevented the negative feelings from entering me during the second half of the song.

Unfortunately, the song was ruined for me when I looked up the lyrics and realized that some of the mumbled lyrics I assumed were about just missing someone were actually alluding to cannibalism and torture methods. This was back in high school, and yet three years later, I heard this ominous song playing on the floor of my residence hall at college! This was both unexpected and disturbing, but nothing I would label as "ominous" actually ended up happening. I do believe in fate, which makes hearing a song that taught me an "everything is not what it seems" message in college seem like more than a coincidence. Maybe I will have a longer story about this in the future regarding what this song was trying to tell me!

Becky G, "Shower" This was playing on the radio when my mom was driving me somewhere years ago, which caused her to ask if I still sang in the shower. I told her no and changed the subject so I would not have to recall the painful memories of that phase of my childhood.

I used to write my own songs and belt them out in the shower every night, but when my dad started commenting on my singing, I got self-conscious and stopped singing in the shower. It didn't matter if I might have sounded good or not; what made me so nervous was the thought that someone had heard me. Literally and metaphorically, I wanted to use my voice as little as possible to avoid attention at all costs. I have worked to overcome that fear since the day of this conversation, but I still refuse to sing in the shower, let alone in front of anyone.

Big Sean's Entire Discography Big Sean's music really hit me hard, especially the songs "Bounce Back," "Light," and "One Man Can Change the World." He is a legend in my mind because he introduced me to a side of rap I had never heard before: a poetic and insightful form of storytelling. His music preaches messages about believing in your worth, rising above hate, staying focused, and so much more. His songs have not been only keys that have unlocked floods of emotions for me because of the powerful lyrics, but also because of the beats themselves. There is something therapeutic about Sean's calm tone mixed with the rhythm of his songs, even the high-tempo ones. There have been countless times where I have been in such an anxiety-provoking, overwhelming situation that I absolutely NEEDED a mental escape, and I that escape has been recalling Sean's raps and repeating them in my head.

I saw Big Sean in concert in the summer of 2017, and it made me cry; a major part of the soundtrack of my life was performed in front of me! The best part was when Sean started singing my all-time favorite, "One Man Can Change the World." Singing along with fellow fans, all from diverse backgrounds but united in song, while waving our hands in the air together made for a moment I can never forget and cannot put into words.

Charli XCX, "Break the Rules" I was the teacher's pet in AP Government to the point where homework assignments were given The Hope Test: if even *I* didn't manage to finish an assignment by the due date, then the due date was extended. This hardly ever happened, since I always did live up to the "teacher's pet" label on accident, taking notes and highlighting on each assignment, due to my obsession with perfectionism.

One day during the last week of school, "senioritis" was rampant. I seemed to be the only senior still paying attention in and doing the work for each class. It was no surprise that I was never asked to join in on the senior prank. The day the prank was carried out, I walked up to the front doors of the school and saw toilet paper and spray paint everywhere, even on our school statue. I entered the school to see the same forms of vandalism throughout the main hallways.

As glad as I was to not be one of the students targeted for detention, a fraction of me felt left out and in the mood to do *something* rebellious. So when my AP Government teacher passed out worksheets, I looked him dead in the eyes, held up my paper for dramatic effect, and ripped it into pieces. The entire class started laughing in awe, but the teacher looked unfazed, shrugged, and said "I'll allow it. She's probably been holding onto this urge all year."

I realize that ripping up paper and refusing to work during one of the last days of school is nowhere near as rebellious as spray-painting a statue, but in my eyes I was suddenly a full-fledged deviant. I walked out of class with "Break the Rules" blasting on the radio in my head, feeling invincible.

Iggy Azalea Featuring Rita Ora, "Black Widow" This was one of the first songs I used to try putting into words how intense my reactions to certain songs are. I told my brother how this song made me feel, and he looked stunned. I didn't realize that not everyone can feel like a song is literally moving them and taking up all of their attention. Didn't everyone else feel like they were getting slowly pushed backwards and then farther and father down a hole throughout the suspenseful "Black Widow" chorus?! Apparently not.

Jacob Whitesides' Entire Discography I had two of my largest panic attacks in the same year of high school. One was during an exam in English class, and the other was during gym class. Both seemed out-of-the-blue, and being startled by them only added to my panic. Anxiety that I experience daily is nothing like a full-blown panic attack: that is an out-of-body experience. My panic attacks involve feeling a numbness all over my body and a sense of suffocation. I cannot move, and my mind feels suspended and unable to do anything but worry about how to reconnect with my body again.

On both days of my school panic attacks, I went home and cried out of embarrassment over the scenes I had caused. Listening to Jacob's music is what calmed me down and helped me forgive myself, especially songs that I personally interpreted as being about staying strong when times are tough. "Focus" and "Hold on Honey" became especially meaningful.

I was blessed to be able to meet Jacob before one of his concerts and tell him this story in person. Mid-story, he pulled me into a hug and told me he loved me. This is an example of a rare time in which I voluntarily was held by someone and appreciated the affection instead of cringing at it. Having my vulnerability feel like it was acknowledged in a way that was compassionate rather than patronizing helped me let down my guard and actually enjoy human contact.

Justin Bieber, "All In It" Despite typically despising physical contact, I still enjoy thinking about hugging and holding hands with my crushes. As young as age eight, I had crushes who I knew I wouldn't mind being comforted by through physical affection. Crushes do not feel like strangers to me, which might be why I don't avoid contact with them as I do with others.

"All In It" was playing in gym class as I scored the winning goal for my soccer team. That was when the unimaginable happened: my crush GAVE ME A HIGH FIVE!!!! After hoping to get at least a glance from him all semester long, I finally got a SMILE, a HIGH FIVE, AND a compliment on my soccer skills! As little as these victories may seem, to someone who has the natural human need for physical contact at least once in a blue moon but also has an aversion to it, an enjoyable interaction like the one with my crush was a THRILL! I had hoped for a hug, but a handshake became a good enough memory for me!

"All In It" played in my head again the other times I refused to interpret the words of crushes as not being flirtatious. These instances were few and far between in high school, but I still vividly remember them because they were rare occurrences in which I enjoyed making eye contact. For example, when one of my crushes, who saw I was wearing a Justin Bieber sweatshirt, drew a picture of someone playing the bongos during class, he showed me the drawing, asked if I like it, and replied before I could with "I bet Justin Bieber plays the bongos." We had such a bonding moment over a possibly false assumption, and it was spectacular!

Lady Gaga, "Born This Way" In school, I watched a panel discussion led by victims of bullying. One of the young panelists talked about his admiration for Lady Gaga and how her music helped him embrace his identity, and he asked if he could sing a little bit of his favorite Lady Gaga song. Of course, the answer was yes, and he belted out the "Born This Way" chorus while beaming and receiving a standing ovation from every single person in the room. I admired him not only for his boldness to sing, but also his bravery to open up about being bullied in the first place. The radio in my head turned off to hear him sing, and I felt as empowered hearing him sing the song as he must have felt hearing Lady Gaga sing it!

Matthew Koma, "Dear Ana" I had never heard of Matthew Koma before I saw promotions for this single on Twitter. I instantly read all about it because naturally, anyone who openly discusses the eating disorder struggles that linger in recovery is someone I want to know about. I remember tweeting him to thank him for such an important and meaningful song about taking back your power instead of letting subconscious forces drive your actions. I was terrified to even post a seemingly vague thank-you note online for fear of the conclusions and assumptions people would make about me, but I luckily didn't get the negative reaction I had been anticipating.

Miley Cyrus, "Can't Be Tamed" When songs feel too loud, they no longer even sound like songs to me. However, the first time I realized that's not the case when I happen to love the song was when I cranked this up and refused to turn it back down. I felt like I was at a concert and felt the entire song energize me more with each second. It was as if I was strutting around a destruction room and all obstacles were getting out of my way just as a result of my intimidating gaze. When someone tried to tell me something and all I could hear through my bedroom door was a muffled sound, it was the ultimate joy for me: "YES!!! It worked!!! I'm really like a normal teenager today!!! I'm just blasting music and not listening to someone!!! I've turned into SUCH a rebel!!!"

MKTO, "Classic" This played every single day I was in the cardio room at my high school for gym class. The repetitive motions and stability I got from using the elliptical were calming, and combining that with music felt like the ultimate therapy. My only unfortunate memory of gym class when this song was playing was from the time I was forced to use a treadmill instead of the elliptical. I spent my Twenty Seconds of Doom holding myself up by the handlebars on the sides of the treadmill, avoiding my feet touching the terrifying bottom part. I gave up and pretended to be fidgeting with the buttons on the machine for the rest of class. That day, I declared the treadmill the scariest and most off-balance device ever invented.

Nick Jonas, "Chains" Typically, I fear even drizzling rain. Rain causes a stinging sensation worse than the one I experienced the time I got stung by a bee. Therefore, the power of concerts to transport me into an impenetrable state of euphoria was fully displayed by the following story:

I watched Nick Jonas perform "Chains" at an outdoor concert venue when a massive downpour started. When I would normally be sprinting towards shelter at a mere raindrop, being surrounded by carefree people and whisked in the mental world of good music made me downright giddy. I simply put on my rain poncho, thanked God that I was sitting halfway under an awning, and couldn't stop laughing as the rain felt like it was hitting me in perfect timing with the music. No stinging sensation was felt, just a sense of being very awake.

Nicki Minaj Featuring David Guetta, "Turn Me On" If I could love anything almost as much as music, it would be trampolines. The in-the-air moments are my equivalent of an adrenaline rush, especially when combined with music. "Turn Me On," for reasons unknown, played during my little sister's party at a trampoline park. I snuck away from the chaos among her friends that was causing my massive headache and found a corner with trampolines that no one was using. For a few fleeting minutes, I was alone and able to jump in-tune with music while no one was watching me, which was a dream come true! Unfortunately, my joy got cut short as a staff member found me and yelled at me that no one was allowed in unsupervised areas at that time. I was angry enough to hurl obscenities his way, but I didn't want to make a fuss and went back to being invisible among my sister and her guests.

OMI, "Cheerleader" My friend Aidan was diagnosed with brain cancer during our senior year (or at least, that's when he made the news public). He died about a month before graduation. At the funeral, multiple family members talked about his love for the song "Cheerleader." It never failed to cheer him up, and he dedicated it to his best friend, whom he had met in the hospital. They went through their cancer treatments together, and he always called her his cheerleader. The "cheerleader" delivered a moving speech at the funeral as well, keeping the focus on joyful memories she had made with Aidan. I instantly saw why he had liked and leaned on her. As the guests, including me, started filing out of the building, "Cheerleader" played over the speakers as I cried.

***Pitch Perfect* Cast, "When I'm Gone"** I was very proud of myself for learning the "cup routine" that goes along with the movie and this song; it was what everyone seemed to want to master at the time. I even chose the "cup routine" as my topic for an instructional speech in English class! The rhythmic feeling of moving the cups through repetitive motions was calming to me, even when I challenged myself to do it faster and faster each time. I actually enjoyed my classmates watching my presentation and applauding, maybe because their eyes were focused on my hands and not my face.

Queen, "Bohemian Rhapsody" My high school pep rally once held live auditions for Prom King and Queen, and the man in the senior class with the deepest voice sang "Bohemian Rhapsody" for the talent portion. I normally curled up into a ball and pretended to be somewhere else during pep rallies, so to have someone be entertaining enough to bring me back to earth by choice was a notable rarity! I'll never forget being awakened from a daydream to see someone burst out from behind an inflatable door and sing in what came across as a Darth Vader impression.

Rae Sremmurd, "No Flex Zone" I started off one summer break with going to see The Weeknd in concert. The show was absolutely captivating to me, hearing one of the smoothest voices in music sing some of my favorite songs after rising out of a futuristic, glow-in-the-dark contraption. I truly felt swept away into another planet!

One of the best parts of the night was even before The Weeknd took the stage, when the rap duo Rae Sremmurd performed. No one was in a high-up row behind us, so my dad suggested we move there so I'd feel less crowded. Once we moved, I felt like I was in a zone where no one could see me and acted as if that were true. I danced and spun around so much that when I looked back at my dad, he was across the arena; I had subconsciously gone from dancing in place to moving far down the empty aisle! Even more out-of-character, I felt no embarrassment and just danced right back over!

Rixton, "Me and My Broken Heart" This played while I was in a tent at a rummage sale. I remember the moment because it was one where I was so worried about the future that I forced myself to focus on my surroundings in the present to avoid panicking. Focusing on the present moment became a coping mechanism for daily life after discussing it in therapy, although I still struggle with this skill today.

Sabrina Carpenter, "The Middle of Starting Over": I wrote in-depth about what this song means to me for an English paper in high school. The song hit very close to home for me, and although I could have written a tear-jerking, extensive submission, I felt too vulnerable to do so. Instead, I described the song's metaphors while omitting any personal connections to them.

If I felt like the teacher grading my paper would have understood what I meant when saying that some music gives me extreme physical and mental reactions, I would have described how "The Middle of Starting Over" felt like I was slowly twirling in circles. It was as if life was in slow motion and I became a calm observer of my environment.

Taylor Swift, "Wildest Dreams" This was another song that played as I slowly left Aidan's funeral. I can no longer hear this song without a subsequent breakdown.

The funeral itself was overwhelming for several reasons. First of all, my own reaction of shedding visible tears scared me; I was not used to external emotional expressions when by myself, let alone in front of many peers and teachers. Second of all, I sensed the bottomless sorrow in every individual and the odd, counteractive forces trying to lighten the mood and force people to laugh as we reminisced about happy times with Aidan. I felt confusion as to which feelings were "the right ones" for the time and which of them were not, but I do remember at the end of the ceremony being grateful that I went. I got to truly *see* my peers, and my sadness felt lessened in the room while we all shared it.

Wiz Khalifa Featuring Charlie Puth, "See You Again" This was the soundtrack to hundreds of late-night car rides one winter. I remember always spending the times the song was on the radio thinking about loss. I thought about Aidan, about various aunts and uncles, about thousands of hospital visits leading up to the death of my grandpa, about the significant percentage of my life so far I had spent seeing ill people, about funerals...I interpreted the song to mean re-visiting loved ones in Heaven, and I remember feeling shocked when my brother said he had assumed it was about a much less morbid topic. The times I heard this song reminded me that not everyone thinks in terms of death as often as I do, yet listening to this song never made me feel sad so much as it did empty.

<u>Part Five: The College Years So Far</u>

Introduction

I don't know if the following story qualifies as bullying and/or harassment, but that is how it felt to me, due to being sensitive and taking everything personally. I preface with this statement to clarify that this person (who I call "Peter") is now gone from my life and does not need to be dealt with by anyone. I would prefer to leave what happened in the past.

Cafeterias are overwhelming due to the crowds and noises coming from every direction, but luckily there aren't many early birds on a college campus, so going to breakfast in the cafeteria was a quiet and tolerable experience. However, I still needed that time away from others, so I always chose to pull out a book or some homework and look busy while sitting alone in a corner. Out of the blue one day, I got startled when someone yelled "HEY!" I said "Hey" back and returned my attention to my book. Usually, this is when the person who tried to enthusiastically start to talk with me gives up, but not Peter. He leaned over the counter in a way that was much too close for comfort, especially given the fact he looked at least a foot taller than me and seemed to be able to go without blinking for an alarming amount of time. He proceeded to ask me about what grade I was in, what classes I was taking, and several other topics. I kept replying in the shortest ways I could and averted my gaze, but Peter either did not take the hints or just assumed I was shy and was actually adoring his company.

After at least twenty minutes of what felt like being in the speed round on *Family Feud*, Peter asked "So what do *you* want to know about *me*?"

Why you won't shut up and leave, I thought, but I went with "Why did you decide to talk to me?"

Peter replied with some rambling sentences about how it's "the right thing to do" when someone is alone to go and talk to them and how he was trying to "be a better Christian."

At this point, since I knew Peter had no intention of leaving, I figured I would talk more instead of less; it would at least distract me from the fact that he stared more intensely than anyone I had ever met. I asked what kinds of clubs the campus had, and that was a mistake. He said that he didn't know much about that due to spending all his free time doing church-affiliated activities. He finally left after a rant about the benefits of converting to Catholicism.

Morning after morning, Peter sat by me at the cafeteria counter, no matter how busy I made myself look. One of two things would happen each day, depending on my mood: either I stayed quiet in the hopes he would also shut up, only to be told in-depth Bible stories and be encouraged yet again to join his church, or I asked questions in response to his religious rants to break his endless eye contact. It was a bonus whenever I asked a question that made Peter lean back to reflect on how to answer, since he otherwise enjoyed hunching over the counter in a way that left little room between us.

To be clear, I was not uncomfortable with the constant Catholic preaching and apparent conversion attempts because of the religious context; it was the persistence combined with the intimidating mannerisms that got on my nerves.

Whenever I tried steering the conversation away from religion, Peter somehow found a way to bring it back around to the only topic he seemed to want to discuss.

Things got creepier when the conversion attempts took on more forms. Peter started detailing not just Bible stories, but also Catholic ceremonies, making sure to point out which ones I was "not too old to experience yet." He slammed my arguments when he used religion to defend hateful statements, including his belief that disabled people and women deserve to keep an inferior status in society.

There are three particular incidents that unnerved me the most. One was when he suggested driving me to his church and staying with me for a service. The second incident was when he asked me for my full name, which he used to search for my email address and send me video links to lectures on Catholicism. The third incident was when Peter excitedly raved about an op-ed he had written for the school paper. He kept requesting me to get a copy of the paper as soon as it became available.

When I read the op-ed, it felt like character defamation. I had spent the past few weeks calling Peter out when he tried to justify bigotry with religious context, and I had frequently responded with reminders about how I did not want to officially label myself as part of any particular religion and preferred to simply believe whatever aspects of whatever religious views I found important. Peter's op-ed was all about the problems with not identifying with a particular religion. He argued that in order to be "the best (insert any religious affiliation here)," one must shut out critiques of even the most trivial aspects of that religion's views. In other words, he argued that being loyal to one's religion requires showing no loyalty to any other religion.

I threw that paper in the trash and never was able to pick up an issue again. I was absolutely furious and felt so vulnerable. All I had tried to say was that I wanted to understand and learn from more religions than just Catholicism, and Peter used my words to essentially call me a sinner.

It isn't dramatic to say my first regular interaction with a fellow college student was scarring. My interactions with Peter were the start of a constant internal battle between wanting to express myself in college and wanting to go back to my old ways and stay silent, having had my first chance at using my voice at college be turned into a scary and embarrassing situation.

Aerosmith, "Dream On" I went to an extremely disappointing Summerfest show that consisted of the opening act screaming into a microphone to an apathetic crowd and taking smoke breaks DURING his set. This was followed by a performance from the headliner that only lasted an hour and turned the his music from the deep, meaningful songs I adored into party-ready remixes that hurt my head and crushed the dreams I used to have of seeing him in concert someday. Needless to say, this concert experience did not give me the sense of escapism that I normally got from shows, keeping me in a state of being overwhelmed by the smells, sounds, and crowds overall.

When the show ended, I left the stadium not only upset, but also hyper-aware of how much I disliked being in close proximity to all the other people leaving at the same time. Every sense hit me at once, from the fireworks crashing against my eardrums to the pushing and shoving that felt like it crashed me to the bone. I felt like my sensory system was being attacked by dodgeballs.

I texted my dad about wanting him to pick me up so I could go home, but he responded that Steven Tyler was about to perform at a different stage and we needed to stay for that. The rational part of my mind thought this was only fair; if I got to see a show, he also should. But the irrational part of my mind felt like screaming "DO YOU HAVE ANY IDEA HOW FUCKING LOUD AND CLAUSTROPHOBIC EVERYTHING FEELS NOW? WHEN I SAY I WANT TO GO HOME, I REALLY MEAN THAT I NEED TO BEFORE A PANIC ATTACK STRIKES!" But I kept that inside as I reunited with him and we went to watch Steven Tyler.

I desperately wanted to leave for the next hour, but there was one significant upside that made the night's frustrations worth it: I actually got to hear a song as timeless and iconic as "Dream On" performed live! And yes, the classic high note was included! During most of the show, I felt like the outsider that I was, not being familiar with the majority of the songs, but I really felt that

euphoric sense of true belonging I get from concerts when everyone pulled out their phones in unison to film "Dream On" and hold
their breath in anticipation for the high note.

Alessia Cara, "Here" When asked which song best describes me,
this is my surefire answer. I love the unique style of words sung in
such a fast, catchy, and rhythmic way that it sounds like a version
of "soft rap" music, which is a good summary of my busy mind.
Like rap music, "Here" gives me lyrics to focus on instead of
OCD-induced counting or other mental escapes. I especially love
the lyrics, which tell a side of party-scene stories that is often
overlooked: being the wallflower who'd much rather be home
and/or alone than in the middle of a "wild night out."

Audien Featuring MAX, "One More Weekend" To say that
Halloween is hard for me is an understatement. My social anxiety
gets to the point where on years when I trick-or-treated, I struggled
to say "thank you" to anyone who complimented my costume. On
years when I stayed home and therefore was obligated to help pass
out candy, I was so easily jolted by the doorbell and so nervous
facing strangers that instead of just staying near the front door
waiting for trick-or-treaters, I ran upstairs to my room, ran back
down whenever someone came for candy, then ran back to my
room, again and again.

Seeing MAX in concert was very special to me because it
was on Halloween. To go to my ultimate source of escapism, a
concert, on one of the hardest days of the year was surely fate; I
felt like I was reclaiming my right to enjoy a holiday for once! It
was also special because of the incredible feeling of belonging that
I get from concerts. That was taken to another level as my fellow
MAX fans and I expressed ourselves fearlessly, wearing head-to-
toe costumes and dancing all night. This was the only Halloween
party I have ever been invited to, but also the best one I could have
ever gone to!

Bebe Rexha, "Bad Bitch" I left math class one day after finishing a test and believed it was fate that this badass anthem came next on shuffle as I walked out of the building. Walking in-tune to such a fierce song made me feel visible, yet not scared of the visibility. I did not just feel like I belonged where I was; I was *owning* where I was!

Bebe Rexha, "I'm Gonna Show You Crazy" During Bebe's concert, she brought a fan onstage whom she had met at a VIP meet-and-greet earlier that day. Bebe said that the fan, who I will call "Heather," had fallen into a deep depression and considered suicide, but she put "I'm Gonna Show You Crazy" on a loop and got through the mental anguish at its worst. This song truly saved her life. Bebe sang part of it while keeping an arm around Heather, and she ended the performance by reminding Heather of just how strong and beautiful she was. Heather cried tears of joy and relief the entire time, and the whole crowd started chanting her name as she left the stage and rejoined the crowd.

This scene was an extremely strong reminder to me of why I love music so much, why I love concerts so much, and why I wrote this book in the first place. How Heather felt about Bebe's music is how I feel about certain artists: their music has truly saved my life. People are not being dramatic by developing strong appreciation for celebrities nowadays; stars' music can pull us through the toughest of times. Singers can be there for you when no one else seems to be, and they can understand you when it seems like no one else does. I felt a connection with Heather that night and with her ability to turn to music to heal her pain.

Cardi B, "Be Careful" This was playing over speakers at SummerFest one night, and I felt so uncharacteristically bold that I yelled out "I LOOOOVE CARDI B!!!" and didn't even care that I got some stares and disagreement from the people around me. I do not get a noteworthy reaction from hearing this song; I chose to include it in this book because I remember the fearless moment so vividly and aim to have more moments of fearless expression in the future!

Dua Lipa, *Dua Lipa* (Full Album) Because I planned to see Dua at a general admission venue, to avoid panicking in the crowd, I got an Early Entry ticket. However, due to popular demand, the show moved to a bigger venue. My Early Entry ticket remained valid, but the staff at the new location didn't know what to do with the people who had bought those tickets from the other venue. So security just let me in to avoid making a fuss over it! Because the full VIPs were busy meeting Dua, and I guess the other Early Entry purchasers didn't bother to ask if the offer still stood for them, I walked into a practically EMPTY VENUE AND GOT A FRONT ROW SPOT!!!! ABOUT A FOOT AWAY FROM THE STAGE!!!

I knew it would be worth it to deal with being in a crowd as long as I was in my happy place: where live music is. The best moment of the night was during a song when Dua walked right over to and smiled at me! I had not only been seen by someone I idolize whose music has given me so much confidence, but I had shared a special moment that not many others got! I felt unworthy but so grateful to have been granted her attention even for a second! Dua represents the fact that we are all enough for anyone worth having in our lives. Dua reminds me that confidence is not the same thing as arrogance and is worth working on having and maintaining. I will always be grateful for the impact her music and live show have had on my self-esteem.

Jason Derulo, "Ridin' Solo" When music that has a negative effect on me has the volume turned all the way up, it no longer sounds like an intelligible song; it sounds like feedback from a microphone mixed with television static. That sums up my mind at the carnival one year, when "Ridin' Solo" blasted. I could not even enjoy the rides I normally do, such as the one resembling a swing set because my pounding headache took over my mind.

Kendrick Lamar, *DAMN.* (Full Album) Listening to fast-paced rap is a rush, yet also therapeutic, giving me something to focus on when "the real world" is unbearable at the moment and I need to immerse myself elsewhere. Thanks to my noise-cancellation headphones and this album, I ignored 5 a.m. football practices, which consisted of high-volume music, shouting, whistle-blowing, and horns. Kendrick's album was a savior those mornings; I would have definitely had a panic attack with all the overwhelming noise outside of my headphones if I hadn't had *DAMN.*'s layered meanings, sounds, and lyrics to distract me.

Lana Del Rey Featuring The Weeknd, "Lust for Life" the shortest way to explain how this song makes me feel is in one word: HORMONAL. I spent many nights playing this song on a loop while letting my mind wander about all things hormonal. It never fails to confuse me that people cling to stereotypes about Autism affecting relationships. According to textbook stereotypes, I apparently have no understanding of or interest in intimate relationships with others. I'm shy, not an unfeeling hermit! As ironic as it may seem, with me not liking to be touched, I still feel very strong desires to be held on occasion, and more intimate desires than just hugs too.

Niall Horan, "This Town" I have only had a handful of voluntary hugs in my life, and one of them was on this night. On the way home from my sister's birthday party, she let me hold her massive teddy bear that a friend had given her. I had wanted one ever since I was very young but had never gotten one, and as silly as it may sound, it was enough to make my day just hugging a teddy bear. I've heard about hugs reducing tension, but since they just spike my anxiety most of the time, hugging a stuffed animal was a great alternative! My sister let me hold Charles the whole ride home, and I was so excited that I made the bear sway back and forth as "This

Town" played on the radio. I could even let go of my self-consciousness enough to make the bear wave at passing cars!

Sam Hunt, "House Party" I had a frankly disastrous first weekend at college. It was even worse than imaginable, starting off with a pep rally. I was separated from my parents and shoved into a front-row seat in a gymnasium, right next to the marching band. I wanted to cover my ears and run out of the gym screaming but got too self-conscious, as usual. I tried to avoid crying in front of so many people, but I likely had tears slip out anyway once guest speakers got off the stage and sat directly parallel to me. I felt their eyes on me as if I was being burned, which only made me want to cry more, yet I couldn't cry more without causing them to keep on staring!

After the horrendous assembly, I found my parents outside the building and burst into very long and loud tears. The feeling of so much noise and so many people surrounding me, combined with the sensation I got from the staring, was unbearable. I wanted to go home, but less than five minutes after reuniting, I had to say goodbye to my parents again.

The next day, I luckily had an aid with me to avoid another meltdown, or to at least distract people if I did break down again. The day's schedule included an afternoon of "bonding" at a ropes course. Every activity revolved around group work, naturally, but also physical contact with teammates. Whether it was trust falls or wheelbarrow races, everyone had to periodically touch each other. After participating in one or two games, I couldn't take it anymore and got my aid's permission to go on a walk. I purposely took my time but eventually forced myself to return to the group to avoid worries about my whereabouts. The sight I returned to terrified me: my aide and the ropes course instructor looked unhappy with one another as they talked about me, my aide fighting for my right to not do what was making me uncomfortable and the instructor (talking too loudly for a private conversation) questioning why I deserved such a "privilege" to exempt myself. He showed complete ignorance towards those with Autism and/or anxiety issues.

Before the next few activities, the instructor announced to the class that I had "issues not everyone has" and therefore would be an unenthusiastic partner. That was clearly not the message I had wanted him to get from talking with my aide. I had known the people I was going to spend the next four years with for less than twenty-four hours before my fresh start was ruined by being called the "one with issues."

Each activity followed a pattern: the instructor told me I didn't have to join in, I backed up and watched, I was told by the instructor to at least "give it a try" after just a few minutes of being undisturbed, I felt pressured into joining, I had to be touched by strangers, and then I retreated again, wanting to dissipate. The worst was yet to come, unfortunately.

The last activity was an "Ultimate Trust Fall." A small picnic table was put on top of a large picnic table. We were supposed to take turns standing on the highest picnic table and then falling off to allow our peers to catch us. As if that was not terrifying enough, the instructor chanted for me to volunteer until the others joined in the chanting. I had never blushed harder and wanted to disappear more. I stood frozen in fear and kept shaking my head. The instructor eventually told me "If you don't do it, you have to nominate someone else to do it." So my choices were to either risk getting killed or risk someone else getting killed who I had nominated! I just kept shaking my head, but he wouldn't stop staring until I made a decision (apparently shaking my head firmly was not considered a decision). I picked my aid to volunteer, which got unexpected laughs that just made me blush harder. She luckily did the trust fall unscatched, but I was an emotional wreck watching it.

I cried so much that night and was so ready to leave that school and never go back. But I cranked up my music and somehow got through the night.

The final "fun" planned for incoming freshmen was a required fancy dinner. I listened to too-loud speech after too-loud speech, followed by a too-loud loop of "House Party" as a slide-show of college memories upperclassmen wanted to share played. I can't listen to "House Party" without thinking about my weekend of Hell at college and all the ignorance towards my special needs that took place.

Now that it has been a couple of years since that weekend, I am honestly grateful for it; nothing college life throws at me seems harder to deal with by comparison! Therefore, I don't necessarily feel scarred by "House Party" playing; I try to think of the times I hear it as opportunities to be proud of making it through that time and years of weeks at college since then!

Shinedown, "Cut the Cord" Some songs stop me in my tracks and either make me feel like I'm on a cloud or plunging down a hole. This song is an example of the latter extreme. It pushes down on my shoulders and makes me feel like I'm sinking. The sinking feeling only got worse when it would play during a car ride and my dad and brother would absolutely refuse to switch it "just because I don't like the song." Many car rides induced even more anxiety in me than usual thanks to this song.

Part Six: KPop and My College Experience

When someone made fun of my change in music taste and love for KPop, I wrote this essay as a way to vent in a way I wouldn't regret:

Discovering music that speaks to me more than ever before has forced me to open up the bottled-up emotions and thoughts I've hidden from the world. What finally enabled me to face my emotions head-on: seeing and listening to KPop music and shows. As strange and silly as that may sound to people unfamiliar with the KPop universe, language barriers are nonexistent when in the presence of songs and music videos that convey the feelings all humans relate to through their delivery. In other words, I feel like I know and can appreciate what is sung even when it's in Korean. KPop pulled me away from the edge of a metaphorical cliff where I had stood while endlessly feeling an implosion. KPop reminded me of how I can relate to others regardless of what seem like barriers, how I deserve to live the human experience with all its complex and mixed-up emotions, and that I am *someone*. I went from not knowing how to feel and express emotions to embracing all of them with open arms. I started to *embrace* the times where I reflected on bad memories, the nights where I cried for hours, and the mornings where I woke up feeling inadequate and too anxious to face the world. Once KPop became the soundtrack along with these routine scenes in my life, the experiences were ten times less daunting. KPop has been there to remind me I am *human* and that all tough times shall pass, with no tough time being too hard to handle. KPop has uplifted me when I haven't smiled in days and has motivated me to set goals for myself while also going easy on myself when they don't come to fruition.

I've always felt the least judged and the most included in concert environments, but the KPop concert environment is a level of unity and joy that far surpasses all others. I don't feel like I'm only showing half of myself, the part that listens to English music; I can show myself 100 percent, the person who listens to music in different languages and doesn't find it odd to benefit from the latter more than the former. Also, to hear a song I love performed live is exciting, but to hear a song that has been my companion during dark times performed right in front of me is an experience too wonderful and cathartic for words to do my reaction justice.

Thank you Stray Kids, for being the soundtrack to my days of punching pillows and feeling the need to have my aggression come out of me. Thank you The Rose, for being the soundtrack to my days of longing and sorrow. Thank you Monsta X, for bringing me a comforting distraction through your music. Thank you SHINee, for being the soundtrack to my nighttime cry-fests. Thank you GOT7, for making music that cheers me up when I need it to the most. Thank you Blackpink, for reminding me I deserve to think highly of myself and am allowed to keep my sassy side. Thank you Day6, for letting me headbang and play the air guitar whenever I've needed a mental escape from my current mindset. There are so many more groups and solo artists I could thank, but the point is they've all captivated me with their visuals and songs, taking me into another world when my real world feels too overwhelming to bear. Hopefully, I will feel overwhelmed to such an extent less and less often as I incorporate the lessons about confidence and individuality taught to me by KPop artists into my daily life, and as I continue to use KPop listening sessions as a coping strategy for life with several anxiety disorders.

The next time you trivialize or criticize someone's music taste, take a moment to remember that the music they love could be much more than music to them. It could be their savior, the final piece in the puzzle needed to make them feel whole. No one has the right to tear apart another's puzzle pieces, and all who fail to recognize the power of music are doing themselves a disservice.

So here is what a day in my life during college is like now:

I have a KPop song stuck in my head as I go through the motions of my morning routine, and although I still grow instantly nervous if someone runs into me and says hi in the dorm halls or if my morning routine's timing gets thrown off-track, the song in my head distracts me enough to make my pet peeves bearable.

Classes still feel intense and nerve-wracking, but I walk to class with my headphones and music on, or at least a catchy song playing in my head. I try to focus in class as best I can, but when I need a moment because I feel like too much is being thrown at my senses at once (for example, when bright lighting is mixed with loud talking), I take a moment to go to a happy corner of my mind, where I relive funny memories from KPop stars' TV shows or their choreography from a performance.

I have lunch in the cafeteria, which is naturally bustling and nerve-wracking. But I always find my corner seat at the counter unoccupied, and I head towards my self-assigned seat while I listen to my music and trying to think of nothing else. If someone stops me on the way to my spot to say hi, I feel good enough to reply and possibly even ask them some questions, knowing that forces me into extending the conversation but also knowing it's the polite thing to do.

After a long day of work, I force myself to spend some alone time in my room watching a handful of KPop music videos and performances. Because repetition is so calming to me, I often go back to watching the same videos, but I force myself to enjoy new content when it is released too. A house party could be going on across the hall and I would simply not care as long as I'm in my KPop World. In that world, my ears can only focus on the music, my eyes can only focus on the aesthetics and mesmerizing dances, and any physical reactions caused by my anxiety, such as my muscles tensing up, seem to disappear.

I still have a complicated relationship with the concept of sleep, but it's less scary once I listen to the same songs every night:

"Elevator" by Jonghyun and "OUR PAGE" by SHINee. Jonghyun is a member of SHINee always and forever, but not everyone uses the present tense. He passed away, and listening to his music helps me feel like he did not. Sometimes it even makes me think that maybe I can convince myself Aidan did not pass away our senior year of high school. Perhaps I can convince myself altogether that death is a false concept. Whatever the case may be, I feel an odd sense of connectedness to the world and hopefulness after listening to Jonghyun's and SHINee's songs before going to sleep.

B.A.P's Full Discography
Trigger Warning: This story includes details of self-harm.

I have always been the opposite of scared when seeing injuries on myself. They don't upset me; they simply cause me to stare at them while zoning out and feeling numb. My mental chaos sees a reason to quiet down when I take a break from feeling so emotional and can just go numb by staring at injuries. Why is something I don't know how to answer.

I've never intentionally cut myself, but I have gotten satisfaction after getting cuts and not tending to them. I used to get satisfaction from not putting bandages on paper cuts until it got to the point where blood smeared the paper, from not putting lotion on my hands when they were dry so I could watch them crack and bleed, and from cutting myself while shaving and just watching the blood flow down the shower drain.

Some days, I got so nervous that I dug my nails into my hand cracks and clawed back the skin to gain the numbness I craved. I had the urge to do this one night when I tried to stop myself and watch music videos as a distraction. I started with the "Wake Me Up" music video and watched one main character, a girl seemingly around my age, break a mirror, smear dark lipstick all over her face as if she was bleeding from her mouth, and start crying. The rest of the video was filled with equally attention-grabbing images of people in pain, until they teamed up to turn their lives around.

I saw myself in the girl from the music video and felt so shocked when forced to reflect on how I had been hurting myself. After spending every night over the next few weeks re-watching the "Wake Me Up" video and watching other B.A.P videos with powerful social commentary, it became routine for me to turn to those videos when feeling triggered to hurt myself. Except for a few relapse moments, I have stared at my injuries with sorrow as opposed to numbness. B.A.P helped me see value in taking care of myself. When I feel so overpowered with simultaneous emotions that I crave numbness, I watch B.A.P videos and feel invigorated, *embracing* being an emotional person and craving a sense of power and self-worth over invisibility. I cover up my cuts right away and use hand lotion now, and although those forms of self-care might seem minor, to me they are large steps towards both internal and external acceptance.

BTS, "IDOL" I used to make video diaries on my iPod Nano, and it was not only a way to feel like my own therapist, but also a way to watch myself and over-analyze how I must come across based on what I saw on film. The videos helped me confirm that I am a terrible singer and dancer (at least when it comes to freestyle). However, I did see in myself the ability to tell stories in an interesting way, which motivated me to keep making the videos. I even considered putting them online to share my stories and advice with the world someday.

I got into an argument with my little sister one day over scrapbook paper. I had only a few pages left and was saving them for a new art project, but my sister wanted them for her own use. I said no, and she decided to serve payback in the most humiliating way she could. She decided to "borrow" my iPod and not give it back for the rest of the day, and because I feel panic set in when people scream or otherwise express signs of a conflict, I just gave in and hoped the day would end soon.

When I ran into my dad a few hours later, he was grinning while saying, "Emma showed me all your iPod videos. They're really funny!"

I had never blown up at my sister quite like I did after hearing that. I was so private at a young age that someone saying "I saw a letter addressed to you in the mail" would have been enough to make me blush and feel exposed; imagine how I felt hearing that both my dad and my sister had learned everything I had vocalized in my diary, not to mention they had heard my horrible singing and watched my awkward dance moves. To top it all off, I had never been trying to be funny, making my dad's compliment quite the opposite.

I screamed through tears at my sister for not only stealing my iPod, but for binge-watching my videos and then sharing them. I scared myself due to my fear of loud noises and made myself blush due to my fear of crying in front of others, so I ended up just yelling more and crying longer. I felt so ashamed that I never made another video diary and never sang or even hummed again, either in public or in private.

Flash forward to this past summer, and I was a 20-year-old eager to try out the "Idol Challenge," which involved dancing to the song "IDOL" and uploading the video. Contest winners would be in a montage video of fans dancing, which would be added to a remix of the video. The concept excited me so much that I was this close to entering and not caring about how silly I looked and felt. But I never entered because of the shame I still have over the video diaries. If my own dad and sister laughed at my dancing when it wasn't supposed to look funny, I couldn't have the entire world see me dance, let alone BTS!

My point in sharing this story is to remind readers that invasions of privacy cannot be brushed off easily by sensitive people. Remember that what you do to "get even" with someone can still hurt them over a decade later, especially when the harm caused is linked to someone's anxiety and therefore can be a memory triggered again and again.

BTS, "Magic Shop" When BTS discussed this song during a press conference, I was intrigued from the start. The song was inspired by the book *Into the Magic Shop* by James R. Doty. I bought the album that includes "Magic Shop" (*Love Yourself: Tear*) and read the book as soon as possible. Without giving too much away, I will say that reading the story about a boy who was mentored by a magic shop worker about the magic within him once he allowed himself to be vulnerable was anything but cheesy. It is a memoir, but to me it is also a textbook for how to understand connections between my feelings and my physical responses and an advice book about how to keep those physical responses from feeling overpowering. Reading the book taught me techniques for how to be conscious of my emotions more often and how to prepare to cope with the physical reactions I can expect from them.

During the press conference, a member of BTS told the audience that he hopes the song is a reminder that when fans are feeling overwhelmed, they can always mentally enter "The Magic Shop" and know there will be seven people there to comfort them. One of my go-to strategies for avoiding panic attacks now involves his reminder. When I know I am about to enter a panic-inducing environment, I prepare myself for the physical responses that go with my panic and act accordingly. For example, when I was at my sister's dance recital this past spring, I learned where the exit doors and bathrooms were before entering the packed auditorium. When I started to feel more nervous than usual and started to anticipate the sensation of my sides closing in on me, I avoided reaching a peak stage of panic by spending time in the building's empty foyer and bathroom. The whole time I power-walked out of the room and tried to calm down outside, "Magic Shop" played in my head, and I tried to block out all thoughts but the visualization of BTS in the mental "Magic Shop". The song makes me feel like I am being comforted and reminds me that when the outer world is too much to handle, BTS has made an inner world to which I will always have access.

Using the techniques from *Into the Magic Shop* and referring to "The Magic Shop" in my head have not erased my panic attacks, but my panic certainly has decreased in frequency and intensity since discovering them. I am forever grateful to James R. Doty for sharing his story and to BTS for their messages of compassionate and understanding they express through song.

BTS, "Singularity" This music video was released without prior notice one morning, which was already exciting enough, but it also happened to be on a day of the week when I always ran into a fellow BTS superfan! She noticed my BTS merch one day in class, and we've been talking about the band ever since. Considering my past of distrusting people, anything that causes me to initiate a conversation and genuinely want it to continue for a long period of time is a huge positive change.

BTS truly brings fans worldwide together, both in person and online. Discussing the symbols within their cinematic music videos and theorizing about their true meanings makes me feel like I'm a part of a special club with its own language. Being a BTS fan means being in a lifelong family, and I will always be grateful for their videos that have spontaneously been released and caused me to have days spent actually smiling while in conversations with someone!

Epik High, *WE'VE DONE SOMETHING WONDERFUL* (Full Album) iKON and Epik High were my soundtrack during the nights of the Orienta-Shit weekends (see the "Sam Hunt" section for an example). "LOST ONE," "LOVE STORY," and "BLEED" from Epik High were especially helpful songs to feel immersed in while curled up in my bed in my dorm room and allowing myself to think whatever bitter or distraught thoughts I had from my time at college so far. It was healing to hear that it's okay not to be okay.

As for iKON, their *Return* album helped me through my orientation weekends other semesters. iKON's album gave me the perfect duality of songs to get up and dance my bad mood away to and songs to play while just letting my stressed-out thoughts pop into my consciousness and be addressed and let go of one-by-one. The album the key to opening the door to a self-therapy session. The irony of songs that combine cheerful sounds with sad lyrics made me feel like it's okay to not know *how* to feel and that a mix of emotions co-existing is normal and relatable. "Love Me" and "Don't Forget" were especially helpful that weekend.

EXO's Full Discography I planned to spend a weekend home from college starting one Friday, and that Wednesday was when I ran out of my anti-anxiety pills. I figured I would just go two days without them and pick up a refill on the weekend when I was home; I didn't want to inconvenience anyone by making someone send me an overnight delivery or drive hours to my school just to drop off medicine. I was in one of my dark mental states at the time and figured that if I had bad side effects to the medicine withdrawal, I deserved it anyway. I had occasionally skipped a day of medication on accident in the past and been fine, so I assumed one extra day of skipping wouldn't make a difference.

It sure as hell did.

Wednesday was tiring but otherwise not noteworthy, but starting 2 a.m. Thursday morning, shit really hit the fan. I woke up every hour after vivid nightmares and spent the day exhausted, sore all over, dizzy, and dried-out. I looked up the withdrawal symptoms of my medication online, saw that my symptoms were the same as the ones online, wrote a will just in case I died (I wish I was joking; I'm nothing if not paranoid), and spent the day in bed, unable to move much without worrying about fainting.

I remained stubborn and angry with myself, so there was still no chance of me asking anyone to help me feel better. But even though I felt like I deserved to feel ill, somehow feeling bored too did not seem ideal. Confined to my bed, I watched music videos for most of the day. EXO's videos were the ones that I kept going back to, simply because they were the only ones that kept making me smile. The more I watched them and memorized the choreography, the more I smiled re-watching them, and the less guilt I felt over letting myself have a good time during a bad situation.

I NEVER want to promote skipping medication, but I'm simply telling my truth when I say that the days I did taught me an important lesson about self-care. Whenever I have a bad day, I no longer say things to myself like "you deserved it," or "go do more work now to feel like a better, more productive person." I now give myself permission to feel sorry for myself, to take breaks from work to watch EXO videos, and to simply smile and laugh out loud. I went from being so fearful of drawing attention to myself that I tried to keep my laughter silent to watching EXO interviews, performances, and videos while smiling or laughing until I fell on the floor crying and not caring who heard me.

GOT7's Full Discography Being in my fifty-minute classes while handling racing thoughts, getting distracted by every sight and sound, and overall experiencing tension from being in the presence of so many other people is hard enough; taking a J-Term course (a course that takes place in January five days a week for eight hours per day) was quite the recipe for end-of-the-day panic attacks. What got me to truly sigh with relief after feeling like I had been holding in that sigh all day long was my GOT7 playlist. January is now my yearly GOT7 Celebration Month, whether I have a J-Term course that year or not. Spinning around to their cheerful songs is euphoric and has given me something to look forward to during the days otherwise occupied with a dreadful emotional state.

iKON, *Return* (Full Album) See the "Epik High" section for the story.

Jonghyun's Full Discography
Trigger Warning: This story includes depression and suicide.

My anxiety often leads to depressed and/or frustrated thoughts, such as the following from my journal:

"The root of my problem is that life is all about balance, and I'm a black-and-white thinker. It's all or nothing with what I say, do, want, don't say, don't do, and don't want."

"Daydreaming about things that will never happen is pointless."

"Looking forward to things worries me because it means I'm relying on the future too much. But I also have to look forward to things as a coping strategy because sometimes the present moment is too unbearable."

"I feel blessed and therefore guilty to feel sad for myself while living a privileged life."

"I feel like I opened up myself this year, and the emotions that have been trapped for nineteen years just keep flowing out."

"I'm trying to get through tough times by myself to not bother and worry others."

"I'm trying to appreciate each day and live in the moment, but I'm also impatient for the future all the time. I seek contentment and find it nowhere."

"I'm used to burying emotions, so suddenly having them all flow out is overwhelming. I don't know how to deal with it. My mind is all over the place."

"Worrying might be just my distraction from endless discomfort and sadness in my life."

Jonghyun's music feels like I have put on a meditation tape. The minute his music sweeps over me, I feel like I am being held and soothed. I feel broken but not permanently; I feel a sense of hope and the willingness to carry on to see better days ahead. Jonghyun's willingness to be open and honest through music has helped me be open and honest with myself, making his music a crucial component of my Anxiety Coping Strategies Playlist.

When I got a news alert in December of 2017 saying that Jonghyun had died of suicide, I fell onto my knees and couldn't breathe. My hero, my sunshine, and my saving grace had been secretly in so much pain that he took his own life. I felt like a ship whose anchor was ripped away. I am writing this about one year since hearing the news, and I still believe time does *not* heal all wounds. I have the same amount of emptiness in me as I did the day the world lost Jonghyun.

I still turn to his music as part of my coping strategies because I know that's what he would love to hear. The least I can do to repay him for his impact on my life is keep his musical legacy alive. He remains one of my motivations to keep on living, so that I can help spread his messages.

Monsta X, "All In" and "Fighter" College has been and continues to be a transformative experience. I started out as a freshman with no idea what I was interested in doing or if I could even handle four years of an often-overwhelming environment. My initial goal was simply to make it through my college days and get decent grades. As has been the case all my life thus far, staying as invisible as possible while carrying out these goals was ideal.

Things did not go according to that plan. I have taken classes on a wide variety of subjects, from writing to math to sociology to criminal justice, and once I discovered what I felt most passionate about learning and discussing, I started doing things I had never done before. I don't mean to imply that my character changed to the point where I strutted into classes every day ready to lead group assignments and be constantly vocal, but it was that drastic of a change when compared to my former mutism at school. I started contributing to conversations, responding to questions willingly, and even presenting research with confidence! I even began presenting at my school's annual symposium.

After days where I would use my voice, such as symposium days, I went back to my dorm and felt slight pride, but I mainly felt dazed. That had been *me* presenting in front of crowds willingly? *I* had followed professional protocol by shaking hands and engaging in smalltalk with faculty? *I* led an audience Q-and-A session and was confident enough to answer every question? *I* did all that? My way of telling myself "YES, YES YOU DID!!!!" was to relive the scenarios in my mind while listening to my favorite songs. "All In" was one of those songs, along with "Fighter," for making me feel so unstoppable that I was ready to do it all over again (and have since then!)!

Monsta X, *Are You There?* (Full Album) Leaving college does not mean that I leave my nerves there. In fact, sometimes it is less stressful to *stay* on campus as opposed to going home. The hardest weekends to go home are ones when changes in routine happen. For example, if my sister invites a bunch of her friends over to our place unexpectedly, if the furniture in the kitchen gets moved around, or if my mom's work hours get changed, my OCD-rooted thoughts are magnified to the max. I crave a sense of control over my surroundings, so I revert to certain OCD rituals the most often when those surroundings keep changing and I'm unable to stop them. Ironically, OCD habits stop me from feeling helpless, yet I simultaneously make them my master.

My OCD habits are a nuisance, but a much stronger term is needed to describe the impact of change when it also affects my Autism and anxiety issues. For example, my sister having friends over at our house not only triggers my obsessive compulsions, but the loud noise triggers my anxiety, due to having a sensory system that is always on red alert.

Here's a more detailed example of when my Autistic, OCD, and anxiety-related traits intersected: When my family decided to buy a new kitchen table that took weeks to be shipped, I came home from college for a weekend to an empty kitchen. That was not "just a kitchen table" in my mind; that was one of the constants that helped my days feel like they were going according to plan and like I remained in control. Stability is what anchors me, and my panic attacks come when I have the out-of-body sensation that comes with having those anchors let loose.

That weekend, I kept trying to count anything I saw in the house, from pillows to silverware, to preserve a sense of mental order that being forced to go in the dining room had disrupted. The anxiety kicked in everytime someone would interrupt the counting. My OCD was not only angry that I had to restart my counting, but it also worried me by saying that if I just let life run its course without maintaining order via counting, something terrible was going to happen.

My sensory issues were added to my distress due to the dining room's structure. The dining room is like a small echo chamber; family dinners sounded louder than usual from both talking and clinking of silverware, and being so close to touching others' shoulders alarmed me. I was especially nervous whenever someone laid eyes on me because gazes feel more intense the closer to me they are.

One of the nights in the dining room got to be too much for me, with everyone yelling and magnifying my sense of being out-of-control. People kept trying to bring me into conversations, leading to everyone's burning stares and silences that made my muscles tense up in the hopes they would all divert their attention before I had to answer anything. To make things more frustrating, my parents sensed that I was more on-edge than usual and tried to console me with advice about handling my transition back to college after the weekend. They entirely missed the point; my brain felt like it was in flaming shambles *at home*, and in the moment I actually could not wait to pack my bags and get the hell out of there.

With my sensory issues, anxious thoughts, OCD-based tendencies, and overall feelings of being misunderstood and scrutinized, I rushed up to my room and closed the door right after dinner, certain I was about to have a full-blown panic attack.

But then I remembered what I've been using to replace my OCD habits: music. I grabbed my journal, started playing the full *Are You There?* album, and wrote to the speed of the music. For the more fast-paced songs, I just dropped my pen and allowed myself to bounce up-and-down or head-bang, thinking about nothing else but immersing myself in the layers of instruments and lyrics. The "flaming shambles" state of my brain was gone by the time the album ended, and I was left feeling like calm ocean waves had taken over and washed out all my frustrations and nerves. My equilibrium was restored, and my panic attack took a rain check.

This wasn't the first time Monsta X music felt like my saving grace; there have been many other occasions where anxiety triggers, OCD triggers, and Autism-related difficulties combined to form such a chaotic mental state for me that I needed a full mental escape, rushed to a room where I could be alone, and just allow myself to move in-tune with the music. Whether a slow song to sway to or a hyperactive song to jump to, being literally moved by Monsta X's music has and continues to make a world of difference in my life.

Monsta X, "Beautiful" One semester at college had several nights where the fire alarm went off around 3 a.m. or another hour when everyone was asleep. Although it might sound petty to hold big grudges over those false alarms, those nights traumatized me and exacerbated my already-present fear of sleep. My nerves feel like live wires; the slightest shock to my senses is like a poke to those wire that triggers a full-body reaction. If someone yelled outside of my dorm's door, I would have been startled awake but recovered in a minute or two. However, to have a piercing alarm wake me up during a deep sleep is another story. Every time the alarm went off, it was as if my live wires were all succumbing to shock at once. I wasn't experiencing anger or even fear, but existential dread. I assumed a fire would burn the place down and went into one of my panic modes, which consists of running and covering my ears. In my all-or-nothing mind, I truly felt like I had would die each time I was jolted awake by a fire alarm. Needless to say, going to sleep again after these alarms was a lost cause.

At 11 p.m. or midnight from then on at college, I felt such fear of being startled awake and having what felt like a near-death experience that I did whatever I could think of to keep busy. If I had a project due in a month, I figured I might as well get a head start at 11 p.m. that night. If my spotless room had a speck of dust somewhere, I might as well dust the whole place. It was such an internal battle to physically force myself into bed, and then it was another battle to even allow myself to quiet my racing mind. I was terrified of falling into a subconscious state and then have my nerves rattled again at 3 a.m.

After a few months of resisting sleep every night, I was so drained that I racked my brain for a way to calm myself down by 11 p.m. I either had to find a way to fall asleep quicker or quit school, in my black-and-white mind.

I had been turning to Monsta X's music as my escapism during those months, so I figured why not try listening to their music and watching their videos to calm down? Despite their hyperactive sound, anything was worth a shot at distracting me from fears.

The first few nights spent watching Monsta X's performances and music videos calmed me down more than I expected, but the ultimate soothing sensation came when I heard their acoustic version of "Beautiful." Both the versions with and without a studio audience got to me. Hearing "Beautiful" acoustic made my live-wire nerves stop trembling and start feeling like they were slowly moving along in-tune with the music. I could mentally picture my nerves as no longer wires, but slow ocean waves. The harmonies and piano in the song had such an incredible effect on me that I was able to shut off my mind within fifteen minutes after hearing it. I certainly still have my fearful nights, but nowhere near as often as they were before I found this antidote for my nerves.

NCT-127, "Fire Truck" It took me years to learn that my phone was compatible with my brother's Playstation, allowing me to watch YouTube videos through his Playstation on a TV screen. I was ecstatic to discover that I could become immersed in the aesthetics and audio of KPop ten times more than before! NCT, especially the sub-unit NCT-127, is now a go-to band to watch in my home-theater-style setting. I have learned over time not only

the meaning of figures of speech and other forms of expression
that were once hard to interpret, but I also have learned and started
using Internet slang. My KPop "escape room" from the real world
was the first place where I shamelessly yelled out phrases like
"YES, MY KINGS!" and "SLAY!". Feeling like I can fangirl
without limitations makes me feel more like myself than ever
before. I will always be grateful to NCT for making me feel like I
have permission to scream and dance like noone is watching. Even
if not music-related, I encourage everyone to find an "escape
room" or "escape corner" that can be theirs and theirs alone.

The Rose's Full Discography I think it's safe to say I think about
loss more than the average person. I think about ex-friends, my
true friend who passed away from cancer, the deaths of family
members, the hours on hours I spent during the first decade of my
life visiting nursing homes and hospitals, the constant fear I've felt
my entire life of natural disasters and other causes of death that
feel very real and unpredictable… the list goes on and on. It's
likely the reason why I am affected by hearing about tragedies on
the news more than others; while some will hear a sad news story
and then go about their days as if it never happened, I will be stuck
thinking about it and worrying about a repeat event for hours. On
the days where the news has left me feeling especially worried,
sympathetic, and sometimes even physically ill, The Rose has been
my band of choice for my musical medicine. The raw tone to the
lead singer's voice, the guitars, the depictions of sorrow in the
music videos, and the lyrics that often feel like they were written
personally for my situation come together to create therapeutic
listening sessions. As much as I appreciate upbeat music as a
distraction during tough times, I have become more appreciative
over time of music that makes me sit with my dark feelings and
truly process and move past them. Turning off the lights, crying,
and feeling swept away by The Rose's music has helped me feel so
human. I appreciate music that forces me to be vulnerable and
learn to be more comfortable being a sensitive, emotional person.

SHINee, *The Story of Light: Epilogue* (Full Album) I used to do whatever I could to NOT express emotions outwards, feeling like it was internally already disproportionate to the situation. But being a hyper-sensitive, hyper-aware person makes me feel all emotions deeply, and I've become more comfortable over time permitting myself to be this way. I no longer try to hold back tears when I really need to let them flow for hours on end, which often happens when I hear things that trigger memories of the day I learned of Jonghyun's death.

The most impactful trigger that causes me to cry for hours at a time: hearing people speak about death, particularly suicide, as if they're talking about the weather. Even if the they aren't directly speaking to me, and even if they are simply stating something like "I should go buy them a sympathy card because their friend just passed away" makes me feel pained. My mind is blown by the audacity some people have to speak about death casually, while I still can't even say "Jonghyun" out loud without getting choked up and wanting to throw things. Maybe my opinion will change, but it has been nearly a year since Jonghyun's passing and still feels like the part of me that died with him hasn't closed up in the slightest. If anything, the emotional scar is bigger, since people continue to say things that anger me and trigger the memory of falling to my knees and sobbing when I heard the news.

I never met Jonghyun but feel such a strong connection to him through my headphones, as strange as that may sound. His music comforts me when no one and nothing else can do the trick, and for no one to seem to acknowledge the pain his passing created in me that I still carry daily only makes it hurt more.

I am endlessly grateful to SHINee for insisting that they will always be five members, for paying tribute to Jonghyun in many ways, and for staying so strong. I admire their courage more than words can say.

WINNER, "Have a Good Day" As I've already elaborated on, the transition to college was Hell. My anxiety reached new peaks throughout my first semester, and some days I felt so paralyzed by fear that I could not get myself to get out of bed until I turned on music as my motivation. Some days were so nerve-wracking, due to thinking about all the social interactions that would drain my emotional battery throughout the day, that I would had my hand on the doorknob to leave my dorm and start the day's agenda and wouldn't be able to turn it for several paralyzing minutes. What got me to fully open the door and go to class was the sensation of calming waves certain songs wash over me, and "Have a Good Day" was one of those songs.

<u>My Top KPop Song Recommendations</u>

The following lists are by no means comprehensive; to list every single KPop song that has helped me cope with daily struggles would be an endless project. I instead chose to stick to my top ten song recommendations for each category. I excluded the top choices that I have already written extensively about, for variety's sake.

<u>What I Have Turned to…</u>

…When I've Needed to Cheer Up
BigBang, "Fantastic Baby"
BTS, "Euphoria"
Highlight, "Plz Don't Be Sad"
Map6, "I'm Ready"
Pentagon, "Shine"
Seventeen, "CLAP"
Seventeen, "Rocket"
Twice, "What Is Love?"
Wanna One, "Energetic"
WINNER, "Really Really"

…When I've Needed to Give Myself Permission to Be Sad
BigBang, "Blue"
BigBang, "Loser"
BTS, "Awake"
BTS, "Spring Day"
Eric Nam, "Lose You"
Eric Nam, "This is Not a Love Song"
G-Dragon, "Untitled, 2014"
SHINee, "From Now On"
Taeyang, "Darling"
Taeyang, "EYES, NOSE, LIPS"

...When I've Needed to Punch a Pillow and Feel a Release of Aggression
Agust D, "Agust D"
Agust D, "Tony Montana"
Crush, DEAN, and Zico, "Bermuda Triangle"
Pentagon, "Runaway"
SF9, "Shadow"
Stray Kids, "District 9"
Stray Kids, "Hellevator"
Stray Kids, "Mirror"
Stray Kids, "Question"
Stray Kids, "Voices"

...When I Need to not Just Boost My Self-Esteem but Feel like a Total Badass
Blackpink, "Ddu-du Ddu-du"
Blackpink, "Playing with Fire"
Blackpink, "Whistle"
BoA, "Woman"
Girls' Generation, "You Think"
Hyolyn Featuring Gray, "Dally"
HyunA's Entire Discography
Jessi, "Gucci"
Mamamoo, "Egotistic"
4Minute, "Crazy"

...When I've Needed to Calm Down
A.C.E., "5tar"
BTS, "Awake"
BTS, "Serendipity"
Cross Gene, "Dystopia"
DEAN, "instagram"
Highlight, "SLEEP TIGHT"
Lee Hi, "Breathe"

Seventeen, "Say Yes"
Seventeen, "Smile Flower"
Wanna One, "Gold"

...When I Need to Watch the Corresponding Music Videos to Experience the Ultimate Sensory Stimulation and Anxiety Escapism

Astro
B.A.P
BTS
EXO
Monsta X
Seventeen
Vixx
Wanna One

Conclusion

If this book has encouraged readers to do anything, I hope it is to find their sources of musical solace. Connecting with songs can feel like you are being reached out to and comforted, talking with fellow fans of an artist can help you break out of your shell and form positive relationships, and turning to music as motivation can make any obstacle look beatable.

I hope to continue sharing my story no matter how nerve-wracking it gets, so that I can fulfill my life's purpose of helping and inspiring others. With the power of music, I know I can do just that, and I hope that this book is just the beginning of a more empowered state-of-mind and a more successful life than I ever thought possible for myself.

<u>Acknowledgements</u>

Thank you Lynn, for believing in my writing and public speaking abilities since day one, for showing constant enthusiasm and encouragement towards this book, and for reminding me to pat myself on the back when needed.

Thank you to Lynn's team, for also showing nothing but support towards the creation of this book, as well as support towards my other endeavors.

Thank you to the therapists, psychiatrists, and other staff members who have aided my journey of coping with mental illnesses. I wouldn't be here to share my story today if it weren't for them.

Thank you to my College Writing course professor for not letting me shy away from writing my full story in assignments. You helped me gain confidence in storytelling and helped me fear feedback from peers less.

Thank you to my Media Studies and Sociology course professors for helping me discover my true passions and encouraging my further efforts to present my views on those topics. The freedom to express my mind in class is one I do not take for granted.

Thank you to the student who showed me kindness during the middle school assembly I describe in the "Somewhere Over the Rainbow" story. That moment has had a huge impact on my life and led to my final days of middle school being more pleasant than I would have ever expected.

Thank you to Aidan for being a true friend. I hope you can read books in Heaven.

Thank you to Katie, Chelsea, and everyone else who has ever mistreated and hurt me. You shaped me into a stronger person and taught me to recognize how I deserve and do not deserve to be treated. Hurt people hurt people, so I hope you have all healed your own personal wounds. I forgive you all.

Thank you to my sister Emma and my parents, for trying to understand things from my perspective as much as possible, being so patient with me all these years, and viewing my disabilities as "super-abilities" instead. I'm grateful to have grown up in an environment where discussing my conditions was not labeled as taboo.

Thank you Scott, for grammar-checking this book and for not being jealous that my book will probably sell more copies than yours. Also, thanks for the comedic relief during writing breaks. You know *exactly* what karaoke picks I'm talking about!

Thank you to the artists who have truly saved me, pulling me out of my darkest moments, giving me a reason to smile when it was hard to find one elsewhere, and providing me with much-needed escapism through songs and performances. I especially am especially grateful to BTS, Monsta X, GOT7, The Rose, EXO, SHINee, and B.A.P. My inner world would still be dangerously negative if it weren't for all of you.

Thank you Jonghyun, for gifting the world with your music and messages. They constantly remind me that it's okay not to be okay; your songs give me a measure of strength that words are not enough to express. I promise to always keep your legacy alive. You are my angel forever and always. I love and miss you.

Thank you Lily Collins, for giving me the courage to open up about my past with an eating disorder. Had you not opened up about your own past with one in your memoir, I likely would not have felt understood enough to do the same without fearing backlash. You are a true hero in my eyes for being open about your past and staying strong!

Thank you Jessie Paege, for normalizing conversations about mental health in your books and YouTube videos. I am forever appreciative of the way you speak about mental illnesses in a way that helps readers/viewers understand what it's like to live with them without making it sound like mental illnesses solely define anyone.

Lastly, thank you to the readers for listening to my story. I hope it has made you reflect on the power of music, has increased your awareness of what life with my conditions is like, and has overall been a meaningful read about the layers of emotions and traits within everyone. We are all more than the sum of a collection of labels.

CPSIA information can be obtained
at www.ICGtesting.com
Printed in the USA
LVHW041759090419
613523LV00004B/688/P